HOW WE HEAL

A Quick Guide To Healing From Grief, Substance Abuse, Alcoholic And Drug Addiction

Dr. Prisha Aryan

All rights reserved. No part of this publication may be reproduced, distributed, or transmitted in any form or by any means, including photocopying, recording, or other electronic or mechanical methods, without the prior written permission of the publisher, except in the case of brief quotations embodied in critical reviews and certain other noncommercial uses permitted by copyright law.

Copyright © Dr. Dr. Prisha Aryan, 2022.

Table Of Content

Chapter 1: Healing From Grief And Loss

Chapter 2 Healing From Substance Addiction

Chapter 3: Healing From Alcoholic Addiction

Chapter 4: Healing From Tobacco

Chapter 1: Healing From Grief And Loss

There is no right or wrong way to mourn, regardless of the kind of loss you've experienced. You may discover better coping mechanisms, however, by being aware of the many phases and varieties of sorrow.

A normal reaction to loss is grief. When something or someone you love is taken away, it causes you emotional pain. Loss's agonizing anguish might sometimes seem unmanageable. You could feel a wide range of challenging and unexpected feelings, such as bewilderment, guilt, shock, or extreme grief. Grief pain may also interfere with your physical well-being, making it difficult to eat, sleep, or even think clearly. These are normal reactions to loss—and the more significant the loss, the more intense your grief will be.

One of life's greatest problems is learning to cope with the death of someone or something you love. Although the most acute sort of sorrow is often caused by the death of a loved one, any loss may produce sadness, including:

- Divorce or breakdown of a relationship
- Health problems Job loss Financial instability
- The miscarriage
- Retirement
- Loss of a treasured dream Death of a beloved pet
- Severe sickness of a family member
- Loss of a buddy loss of security after trauma
- The family house being sold

Grief may be sparked by even little losses in life. You could experience grief, for instance, if you move away from home, graduate from college, or change careers.

No matter what you've lost, it's personal to you, so don't feel bad about how you feel or think that only specific losses should be mourned. It's common to experience loss and mourn whether the deceased was a meaningful person, animal, connection, or circumstance for you. Whatever your reason for grieving, there are healthy strategies to deal with the suffering that, over time, may lessen your sorrow and assist you in accepting your loss, finding a new purpose, and ultimately moving on with your life.

Few things are as terrible as losing someone you love, whether it be a close friend, a spouse, a partner, a parent, a kid, or another relative. Life may never feel the same after such a tragic loss. But with time, you may lessen your grief, begin to look forward, and ultimately accept your loss.

The process of mourning
There is no right or wrong way to mourn; it is a very personal process. How you mourn is influenced by a variety of things, such as your personality and coping mechanisms, your life experience, your religious beliefs, and the importance of the loss to you.

The mourning process always requires time. There is no "normal" timeframe for mourning; healing develops gradually and cannot be hastened or coerced. In weeks or months, some individuals start to feel better. Others' grief processes take years to complete. Whatever your level of pain, it's crucial to be kind to yourself and let things take their course.

How to handle the mourning process
While experiencing loss and mourning is a natural part of life, there are strategies to ease the suffering, accept your loss, and finally find a way to pick up the pieces and go on.

Recognize your suffering

Recognize that a variety of unanticipated emotions might be triggered by sadness.

Recognize that you will go through a specific grief process.

Ask those who care about you for in-person assistance.

You can support your mental health by looking after your bodily needs.

Know the difference between sadness and sorrow.

Call a Therapist Right Away

Elisabeth Kübler-Ross, a psychiatrist, first described the "five phases of grieving" in 1969. Although many people have applied these phases of mourning to other sorts of traumatic life events and losses, such as the death of a loved one or a breakup, they were originally founded on her study of the emotions of patients facing terminal illness.

Grief's five phases
Denial: I can't be the one experiencing this.

Fury: "Why is this taking place? Who is at fault?
Negotiation: "Make this not occur, and in exchange, I will ."
Depression: "I don't feel like doing anything."
Acceptance: I'm at peace with what occurred.

Following a loss, it may be comforting to know that these feelings are normal and that you will eventually get over them. But it's alright if not everyone who grieves experiences all of these phases. Contrary to common opinion, healing does not need to go through each step. Some individuals can get over their sorrow before they ever reach any of these phases. Don't stress about how you "should" be feeling or whatever stage you "should" be in if you do experience these phases of grieving since you probably won't move through them in a tidy, chronological way.

These phases were never meant to be a set process that all mourners must follow, according to Kübler-Ross. The five phases of mourning, she said, "were never designed to help put untidy feelings into neat packages," in her last book before her death in 2004. Many individuals have these reactions to lose, but there isn't a normal reaction to loss since there isn't a typical loss. As unique as our lives are, so is our sorrow.

We may see the mourning process as an emotional roller coaster with highs and lows rather than a sequence of phases. The ride often has a harsher start, and the low points may be longer and deeper than on other roller coasters.

Although it takes time to recover after a loss, the challenging times should become easier and shorter with time. We may continue to feel intense sadness even years after a loss, particularly on important occasions like a family wedding or the birth of a child.

Even though everyone is affected by loss differently, many of us go through the following symptoms while we're mourning. As you go through the early stages of mourning, keep in mind that practically everything you feel is normal, even feeling as if you're going mad, as though you're in a horrible dream, or as though you're doubting your religious or spiritual beliefs.

Shock and astonishment. It might be hard to accept what transpired right away after losing. You can experience numbness, have problems accepting the loss as true, or even reject reality. For instance, even after a loved one or a pet has passed away, you could continue to wait for them to appear.

Sadness. Probably the most prevalent sign of mourning is extreme sadness. You can experience sensations of emptiness, hopelessness, longing, or extreme loneliness. Also possible are frequent tears or unstable emotional states.

Guilt. You could have regrets or feel bad about something you said, did, or didn't do. Additionally, you could feel bad about some emotions (feeling relieved when a person died after a long, difficult illness, for example). Still, if it was entirely beyond your control, you could even feel regret for not doing more to stop your loss.

Fear. A severe loss might result in a variety of anxieties and worries. You can feel worried, powerless, or apprehensive about the future if you've lost your relationship, your job, or your house, for instance. even get panic attacks. When a loved one passes away, it might make you anxious about your mortality, how you'll manage without them, or how you'll handle your new, independent duties.

Anger. Even though no one was to blame for the loss, you could feel bitter and furious. If you lost a loved one, you can feel upset with God, yourself, the medical staff, or even the deceased for leaving you. You may want to hold someone accountable for the unfair treatment you received.

Grief-related physical manifestations
While mourning often entails physical issues as well as emotional ones, some of them include:

- Fatigue
- Nausea
- diminished immunity
- Gaining or losing weight
- Pains and aches
- Insomnia

Various griefs
It's difficult to categorize any sort of mourning as either "normal" or "abnormal," since the experience of grieving after the

death of someone or something significant to you tends to be personal to you. There are, however, other varieties of mourning that are not represented by the aforementioned anticipated signs and behaviors. These consist of:

Anticipating sadness
Anticipatory sorrow, as the name implies, arises before a severe loss rather than after it. You could begin mourning your loss before it has completely materialized if, for instance, a loved one is terminally sick, a pet is becoming older, you are about to retire or lose your work, or if any of these situations apply to you.

Similar to regular grieving, anticipatory grief may include a variety of contradictory feelings, including rage. Some individuals refuse to allow themselves to mourn before their loss has happened, often equating it with giving up hope. However, anticipatory grieving may also allow you the opportunity to make last preparations, take care of any unfinished business, or say your goodbyes.

Angry disenfranchisement
When your loss is undervalued, stigmatized, or cannot be publicly lamented, you may experience disenfranchised sorrow. Some individuals can dismiss the loss of a job, a pet, or a relationship as something that isn't important enough to express grief over. If you had a miscarriage or lost a loved one to suicide, you could feel stigmatized.

When your connection to a departed person is not acknowledged, you may experience sadness that is not valid. Some individuals may think it's unacceptable to express grief over a friend, classmate, or neighbor, for instance. You may not get the same empathy and understanding as a blood family as a close friend or same-sex partner. This may make it more challenging to absorb your loss and go through the mourning process.

Difficult sorrow

Even while a large loss may never totally remove the anguish, it should gradually lessen. If it doesn't, difficult grieving may be present if it prevents you from getting back to your routine and maintaining your connections.

When a loved one passes away and you are left in a condition of grieving, complicated sorrow often follows. You could find it difficult to go on when your loved one passes away, look for them in familiar places, sense a deep desire, or perhaps think life isn't worth living.

It's crucial to seek assistance and do the things that will help you recover if your grieving is difficult and there is still unresolved anguish from your loss.

You may feel the want to isolate yourself and withdraw from others while you are grieving. But overcoming a loss requires the direct, personal help of others. When you are mourning, it's crucial to communicate your emotions, even if you don't feel comfortable doing so in other situations.

Even while talking about your loss with friends and family might help you cope with your sorrow, you don't have to do it every time you see them. Another source of comfort is just being in the presence of people who care about you. Avoiding isolation is the key.

Consult your family and close friends. Even though you pride yourself on being tough and independent, now is the moment to rely on the people who love you. Draw close to your friends and family, spend time with them in person and embrace the help that is provided rather than ignoring them. Tell them what you need, whether it's a shoulder to cry on, a listening ear, or simply someone to hang out with since sometimes people want to help but don't know how. It's never too late to make new friends if you don't feel like you have someone you can connect with in person daily.

Recognize that many individuals find it hard to soothe a mourning person. Many individuals find grief to be a perplexing and perhaps terrifying feeling, particularly if they haven't personally gone through a comparable loss. They can be unaware of how to console you and say or do the wrong things as a result. But don't use it as an excuse to isolate yourself and shun interaction with others. If a friend or family member reaches out to you, it is out of concern.

Take solace in your religion. Accept the consolation that your religion's customs for grieving might provide if you practice it. You may find comfort in engaging in spiritual pursuits that have importance to you, such as prayer, meditation, or church attendance. In the aftermath of the loss, speak to a clergyperson or other members of your religious community if you're having doubts about your beliefs.

Speak with a therapist or grief specialist. Find a mental health practitioner with training in grief therapy if your sorrow becomes overwhelming. An expert therapist may assist you in navigating difficult emotions and overcoming mourning challenges.

Social media may help share your grief with others and ask for support. Internet trolls who post inappropriate, offensive, or even violent words may be drawn to it, however. You may wish to restrict your usage of social media to private groups rather than public posts that anybody can remark on at this time to save yourself more misery and sorrow.

Taking care of oneself becomes more crucial than ever while you're mourning.

Your energy and emotional reserves may be swiftly depleted by the stress of a significant loss. It will be easier for you to get through this challenging period if you take care of your physical and emotional needs.

Embrace your emotions. Even if you try, you won't be able to escape experiencing sadness forever. You must admit your suffering if you want to recover. Avoiding pain and loss simply makes the mourning process take longer. Complications including despair, anxiety, drug misuse, and health issues may result from unresolved sorrow.

Put your sentiments into words or something artistic. Even if you are unable to discuss your grief with others, writing down your thoughts and emotions in a notebook, for instance, might be helpful. You might also create a scrapbook or donate your time to a charity linked to your loss as a way to express your feelings.

Try to keep up your interests and hobbies. Routine provides solace, and returning to the pursuits that make you happy and knit you to others might help you accept your loss and hasten the mourning process.

No one, even yourself, should be able to tell you how to feel. Nobody else has the right to judge whether it's time for you to "move on" or "get over it" since your pain is your own. Allow yourself to experience whatever you feel without shame or criticism. It's OK to be enraged, to curse the sky, to weep, or not cry. It's also OK to find moments of happiness, to laugh, and to let go when the time is right.

Take care of your physical well-being. The body and mind are intertwined. You'll be able to handle difficult emotional situations easier when you're physically fit. By getting adequate sleep, eating well, and exercising, you can fight stress and weariness. Do not artificially uplift your mood or dull the agony of bereavement with booze or drugs.

Be prepared for "triggers" of sorrow. Holidays, anniversaries, and significant anniversaries might bring up negative memories and emotions. Be prepared for an emotional wallop, and know that it's entirely normal. You may prepare in advance by, for instance, ensuring that you aren't alone or by creatively commemorating your loss.

Chapter 2 Healing From Substance Addiction

Drug addiction is not a sign of weakness or a deficiency in one's character, and overcoming it requires more than just resolve. Drug abuse may alter the brain, resulting in strong cravings and a temptation to use, making abstinence seem like an impossibility. This can happen while taking illicit substances or certain prescribed medicines. No matter how terrible your circumstances appear or how many times you've tried and failed before, rehabilitation is always possible. Change is always achievable with the correct care and encouragement.

The first step toward recovery is sometimes the most difficult for those who are battling addiction: admitting you have a problem and resolving to take action. It's common to question your ability to stop using or if you're ready to begin your recovery. You could worry about how you're going to find an alternative approach to address a medical issue if you're hooked to a prescription medicine. It's OK to be torn. Changing several things is necessary to commit to sober, including:

- How you respond to stress.
- Those people you let into your life.
- What you do while you're not working.
- How you see yourself.
- Your use of prescription and nonprescription drugs.

Even when you are aware of the issues your drug of choice is bringing into your life, it's common to have conflicting feelings about quitting. You can conquer your addiction and take back control of your life by committing to change. Recovery involves time, dedication, and support.

Drug addiction (substance use disorder) diagnosis necessitates a comprehensive examination, which often entails an evaluation by a psychiatrist, psychologist, or certified alcohol and drug counselor. Drug usage is assessed by blood, urine, or other lab tests; nevertheless, these tests do not serve as an addiction diagnostic tool. These tests might, however, be used to keep tabs on therapy and healing.

Most mental health practitioners utilize the criteria included in the Diagnostic and Statistical Manual of Mental Disorders (DSM-5), released by the American Psychiatric Association, to diagnose drug use disorders.

Keep a record of your drug usage, including the quantity and frequency. You will have a clearer understanding of the part the addiction is playing in your life as a result.

Make a list of your drug use's advantages and disadvantages, as well as the costs and rewards of stopping.

Think about the things in your life that are significant to you, such as your spouse, children, pets, profession, or health. How are those items impacted by your drug use?

Inquire about the opinion of a person you trust on your drug usage.

Look within to see whether anything is stopping you from changing. What might aid you in changing?

Steps to change readiness and addiction recovery

Recall the factors behind your desire to change.

Consider any prior efforts you may have made to recover. The solution? What failed?

Decide on clear, quantifiable objectives, such as a start date or medication use restrictions.

Remove all signs of your addiction from your home, place of employment, and other frequented locations.

Inform your loved ones that you're devoted to your recovery and ask for their help.

Investigate your alternatives for addiction therapy

It's time to consider your treatment options after you've decided to pursue recovery. Although the kind of substance used might affect the type of addiction therapy, a good program often consists of many components, such as:

Detoxification. The first stage is often to rid your body of narcotics and treat withdrawal symptoms.

Behavioral therapy. Therapy may assist you in discovering the underlying reasons for your drug use, mending broken relationships, and acquiring more effective coping mechanisms.

Medication may be used to treat any co-occurring mental health issue, such as depression or anxiety, as well as to control the withdrawal symptoms and avoid recurrence.

Long-term follow-up may aid in maintaining recovery and preventing relapse. This can include participating regularly in offline or online support groups to help you stay on the right path throughout your rehabilitation.

Programs for drug treatment by kind
Residential therapy - During intense treatment, patients live at a facility away from their jobs, studies, families, friends, and addiction triggers. A few days to many months might pass during residential therapy.

Day treatment/partial hospitalization: People who need continuing medical supervision but still want to remain at home and have a stable living situation might choose partial hospitalization. These therapy programs often meet for 7 to 8 hours during the day in a treatment facility, after which you go home at night.

Treatment that is provided on an outpatient basis—as opposed to a live-in program—can be planned around obligations such as work or school. You don't remain overnight; treatment takes place throughout the day or evening. The avoidance of recurrence is the main priority.

Communities for sober life - A rigorous treatment program, like residential treatment, is often followed by sober living. You live in a secure, encouraging, and drug-free environment with other addicts in recovery. If you don't know where to go or are concerned that going home too soon could trigger a relapse, sober living facilities might be helpful.

How to choose the ideal drug rehabilitation program for you

Keep in mind that not every therapy is effective. Each person has unique demands. Whether you use prescription or illicit substances, addiction therapy should be tailored to your particular circumstances. Finding a curriculum that feels appropriate is crucial.

Your drug misuse should not be the only issue addressed in treatment. Your relationships, work, health, and psychological well-being are all impacted by addiction. Treatment success relies on creating a new way of life and addressing the causes of your drug use in the first place. In this scenario, you'll need to discover a better strategy to manage stress or alleviate pain. For instance, your drug abuse may have arisen from a need to manage pain or deal with stress.

Key components include dedication and persistence. Treatment for drug addiction is a lengthy procedure. Generally speaking, the length and intensity of your therapy will depend on how long and how heavily you used drugs. Long-term follow-up treatment is essential to recovery in any situation.

There are many locations to look for assistance. Not everyone needs to undergo medically assisted detox or a lengthy stay in treatment. The kind of treatment you need is determined by some variables, such as your age, drug use history, and physical or mental health issues. Numerous church people, social workers, and counselors also provide addiction treatment services in addition to physicians and psychologists.

Concurrently, get therapy for any mental health issues. In addition to getting treatment for your drug addiction, it's critical to address any underlying medical conditions or psychological problems.

Receiving treatment for both addiction and mental health issues from the same team or physician can increase your chances of success in recovery.

Find assistance for your recovery from addiction.
Don't attempt to handle things on your own; seek help. Having a strong support system and good role models is crucial regardless of the kind of therapy you choose. The more opportunities for rehabilitation, the more individuals you can lean on for support, advice, and a sympathetic ear.

Lean on your close relatives and friends. The help of friends and family members is a crucial tool for healing. Consider seeking relationship counseling or family therapy if you're hesitant to turn to your loved ones because you've disappointed them in the past.

Create a network of sober friends. You may need to establish some new relationships if drugs were the center of your former social life. Having friends who are clean and will help you with your recovery is crucial. Consider enrolling in a class, becoming a member of a church or civic organization, volunteering, or going to local events.

Think about relocating to a sober living facility. While you're getting clean from drug addiction, sober living houses provide a secure, encouraging environment to call home. If you don't have a stable household or a drug-free living situation, they are an excellent choice.

Emphasize your meetings. Sign up for and consistently attend meetings of a 12-step recovery support organization, such as Narcotics Anonymous (NA). Spending time with others who completely get your situation may be quite therapeutic. The group members' shared experiences might be helpful to you, and you can pick up tips on how others have managed to maintain sobriety.

Discover constructive strategies to deal with stress.
After dealing with your addiction's immediate issues and beginning treatment, you'll still need to deal with the issues that contributed to your drug consumption. Did you begin using it to mask unpleasant feelings, to relax after a fight, to decompress after a stressful day, or to distract yourself from your problems?

The bad emotions you numbed with drugs will reappear once you're clean. For therapy to be effective, your underlying problems must be addressed first.

Even when your underlying problems are taken care of, you will sometimes still feel stressed, lonely, frustrated, angry, ashamed, anxious, and hopeless. All of these feelings are common human experiences. Your therapy and recovery depend on you learning how to deal with these emotions as they occur.

There are more wholesome approaches to managing your stress. You may develop problem-solving skills to prevent relapsing into your addiction. When you have faith in your capacity to reduce stress rapidly, dealing with intense emotions isn't as frightening or overwhelming.

Some individuals find that some rapid stress alleviation techniques work better than others. Finding the one that works best for you is the key.

Movement. It may be sufficient to take a little stroll around the block to decompress. Another great approach to reducing stress and achieving balance is yoga and meditation.

Go outdoors and enjoy the sunshine and clean air. Enjoy a stunning vista or setting.

Have fun with your cat or dog. Enjoy your pet's fur's soothing touch.

Use your sense of smell to experiment. Savor a perfume that takes you back to a cherished holiday, like sunscreen or a seashell, or inhale the aroma of fresh flowers or coffee beans.

Close your eyes and visualize a serene setting. Consider a sandy beach or a special memory, such as the first steps taken by your kid or time spent with friends.

Treat yourself. Make yourself a hot cup of tea and give your shoulders or neck a massage. Take a hot shower or bath.

Control drug cravings and triggers.
Getting sober is only the beginning of your rehabilitation. The connections in your brain

that altered when you were an addict require time to restore. Drug desires may be strong throughout this rebuilding period. By avoiding others who make you feel the want to use, locations, and circumstances, you may help your ongoing recovery:

Leave your drug-using buddies alone. Avoid spending time with pals who continue to use drugs. Avoid individuals who can urge you to relapse into your damaging old habits and instead surround yourself with those who will encourage your recovery.

Avoid nightclubs and bars. Drinking reduces inhibitions and affects judgment, which may easily result in a relapse even if you don't have a drinking issue. Drugs are often easily accessible, and the urge to use them may be strong. Likewise, stay away from any additional settings and circumstances that you connect with drug usage.

Be honest about your drug usage history while requesting medical care. Find a doctor or dentist that will work with you to prescribe the least amount of medication or other options if you need to have a medical or dental treatment done. Never should you be refused pain medicine or made to feel embarrassed or degraded because of prior drug use; if this occurs, contact another physician.

Use prescribed medication with care. If you were dependent on a prescription substance, such as an opioid painkiller, you may need to discuss pain management options with your doctor. It's crucial to avoid prescription medicines with abuse potential or take them only when required and with the utmost care, regardless of the substance you had issues with. Painkillers, sleeping medications, and anti-anxiety drugs all have significant abuse potential.

Managing drug urges

When cravings cannot be resisted, a coping mechanism must be developed:

Participate in a calming activity. Read, visit friends, watch a movie, indulge in a hobby, go hiking, or engage in physical activity. You'll discover that the desires vanish whenever you're engaged in anything else.

Talk it over. When a desire strikes, discuss it with friends or family. Finding the cause of hunger may be done very well through talking. Additionally, discussing your cravings often can help you release and alleviate the emotion and will help your connection become more honest. There is no need to feel awful about cravings.

Reframe and challenge your ideas. Many individuals tend to forget the negative effects of the drug's use while they are feeling a need and only recall its benefits. Since you stand to lose a lot if you use it, it may be beneficial to remind yourself of this. You won't feel any better as a result. These repercussions may often be helpfully stated on a tiny card that you carry everywhere.

Please surf. Many individuals attempt to tough it out to control their cravings. However, certain appetites are too powerful to suppress. When this occurs, resisting the temptation until it subsides might be helpful. This method is known as urge surfing. As if you were a surfer, see yourself riding the wave of your drug urge and remaining on top of it until it crests, breaks, and transforms into weaker, frothy waves. You'll discover that the urge goes faster than you anticipate if you just ride it out without attempting to fight, condemn, or ignore it.

The first three stages in urge surfing are:
Observe how the desire affects you. Place your hands in a relaxed posture and feet flat on the floor as you sit in a comfy chair. Breathe deeply a few times, then

concentrate on your body. Keep track of the hunger or impulse you are having and where in your body it is happening. Express what you're feeling in words. You may tell yourself, for instance, "My hunger is in my mouth, nose, and stomach."

Concentrate on only one place where hunger is present. What feelings are there in that area? Tell yourself what they're like. Do you, for instance, experience heat, cold, tingling, or numbness? Perhaps you have stiff muscles? How much space is at stake? As you concentrate on the feelings, take note of any changes. My mouth is dry, I feel. My lips are feeling numb. I can visualize the experience of utilizing it as I swallow.

Repeat while concentrating on every area of your body that feels the need. Describe to yourself how the impulse comes and passes and how the feelings alter. Many individuals discover that their need has subsided after a few minutes of urge surfing. However, the goal of this practice is to feel the impulse freshly rather than to make it go away. If you routinely indulge in urge surfing, you'll get to know your desires better and find it simpler to endure them until they pass on their own.

Create a purposeful drug-free lifestyle
Having hobbies and interests that give your life purpose might help you stick with your drug treatment and prevent relapse. It's crucial to become engaged in activities that you find fulfilling, make you feel wanted, and give your life purpose. Your addiction will become less appealing if you have meaningful responsibilities and a feeling of purpose in your life.

Attempt a new pastime or pick up an old one. Attempt things you've always wanted to try that will stretch your imagination and ignite your creativity. Take up a new sport, a foreign language, or a musical instrument.

Take in a pet. Pet ownership comes with responsibilities, but taking care of an animal also makes you feel wanted and appreciated. Pets may also help you get some exercise by getting you outside.

Spend some time outside. Go on a beautiful trek, go fishing or camping, or just go for routine park strolls.

Embrace the arts. Take an art lesson, attend a theater or concert, visit a museum, or write a memoir.

Participate in your neighborhood. Join drug-free clubs and activities to replace your addiction. Join a club or neighborhood organization, volunteer, or become involved in your church or another place of worship.

Set important objectives. Having objectives to strive for and something to anticipate may be effective treatments for drug addiction. What matters is that you value the objectives and that they are essential to you.

Take care of your health. You may maintain high energy levels and low-stress levels by engaging in regular exercise, getting enough sleep, and practicing good dietary habits. It will be simpler to remain clean the longer you can maintain excellent health and mental well-being.

Relapse shouldn't keep you down.
Relapse occurs often throughout the process of becoming clean from drug addiction. Relapse may be depressing and distressing, but it can also be a chance to learn from your errors, find new triggers, and alter your treatment plan.

Why do relapses occur?
You may be in danger of relapsing into previous drug use behaviors due to several "triggers". While individual triggers for relapse vary, some typical ones are as follows:

feeling that is negative (such as stress, sadness, anger, or trauma)

Emotionally healthy condition (feeling happy and wanting to feel even better, such as having a good time with friends)

bodily discomfort (such as pain or withdrawal symptoms)

Test your self-control by saying, "I can use it only once" or "take just one pill."

strong desire or temptation (craving to use)

Conflict (such as a disagreement with your spouse or lover) (such as an argument with your spouse or partner)

Peer pressure (being in a situation where it seems everyone else is using)

It's crucial to keep in mind that recurrence does not indicate that pharmacological therapy was ineffective. Never give up. Call your sponsor, speak with your therapist, attend a meeting, or make a doctor's appointment. Examine what precipitated the relapse, what went wrong, and what you might have done better once you're clean again and no longer at risk. You might decide to recommit to your recovery and make the most of the experience to fortify your resolve.

Chapter 3: Healing From Alcoholic Addiction

Alcoholism, which is another name for alcohol addiction, is a disorder that may affect anybody. Researchers have made an effort to identify risk variables for alcohol addiction, such as heredity, sex, ethnicity, or socioeconomic status. But there is no one reason behind it. The condition may be caused by psychological, genetic, and behavioral causes, among others.

The fact that alcoholism is a genuine illness must be emphasized. Alcoholism may alter the brain's neurochemistry, making it possible for a person to lose control of their behaviors.

There are several ways in which alcohol addiction may manifest itself. Each individual has a unique level of illness severity, frequency of alcohol use, and alcohol consumption. Some individuals binge drink and then abstain from alcohol for a period, while others drink extensively all day.

Regardless of how the addiction manifests, if a person relies excessively on alcohol and finds it difficult to maintain sobriety for a lengthy time, they likely have an alcohol addiction.

Alcoholism might be difficult to identify. Alcohol is easily accessible and tolerated across many cultures, unlike cocaine or heroin. It often occupies the center of social interactions and is intimately connected to pleasure and celebration.

For a lot of folks, drinking is a way of life. When drinking is accepted in society, it may be difficult to distinguish between someone who enjoys the occasional drink and someone who has a problem.

Among the signs of alcoholism are:

Increased alcohol use in amount or frequency, strong alcohol tolerance, or absence of "hangover" symptoms.
Changes in friendships; drinking at inappropriate times, such as first thing in the morning; in settings like church or work; a desire to be where alcohol is available and a tendency to avoid situations where it is not;
Someone who is dependent on alcohol to operate in daily life may choose companions who drink excessively, avoid contact with loved ones, or hide alcohol while doing so.
elevated sluggishness, despair, or other emotional problems
or troubles with the law or the workplace, such as being arrested or losing your job
It's crucial to seek early warning signals since addictions can worsen over time. Someone who has an alcohol addiction may be able to escape serious repercussions of the condition if they are detected and treated early.

It's better to approach someone you know in a supportive manner if you're concerned that they may have an alcohol problem. Avoid making them feel guilty or ashamed. This can turn people off and make them less receptive to your assistance.

What negative effects on health are related to alcoholism?

Alcohol addiction may cause liver and cardiac problems. Both are lethal. Another effect of alcoholism is:

- Ulcers
- Diabetes-related issues
- Sexual issues
- Birth flaws
- Bone loss issues with the eyes
- Elevated chance of cancer
- Reduced immunological response

Alcohol addicts who engage in risky behavior while drinking might endanger other people as well. The Centers for

Disease Control and Prevention (CDC) estimate that 28 people die in the United States each day as a result of drunk driving. Additionally, drinking is linked to a higher rate of murder and suicide.

These issues are the justifications for the significance of early alcohol addiction treatment. With effective long-term recovery, almost all dangers associated with alcohol addiction may be avoided or treated.

What are the alcoholism treatment options?
Alcohol addiction treatment may be complicated. The individual with an alcohol addiction must desire to stop drinking for therapy to be effective. If they aren't ready to quit drinking, you can't make them. Success is based on an individual's drive to improve.

Alcoholism rehabilitation is a lifelong commitment. There is no fast repair, and everyday maintenance is required. Because of this, many individuals claim that alcoholism can never be "fixed."

Rehab

Outpatient or inpatient rehabilitation programs are often used as the first line of therapy for alcohol addiction. A 30-day to 12-month inpatient treatment is possible. It may aid someone in overcoming emotional difficulties and withdrawal symptoms. While enabling the patient to remain at home, outpatient therapy offers daily assistance.

Organizations such as Alcoholics Anonymous and others

Numerous alcoholics seek help from 12-step groups like Alcoholics Anonymous (AA). Other support organizations, such as SMART Recovery and Sober Recovery, do not adhere to the 12-step philosophy.

It's beneficial to join at least one support system while going sober, regardless of the kind. Someone who is battling an alcohol addiction may get support from sober groups to assist them to navigate the difficulties of recovery in daily life. In addition to offering fresh, healthy connections, sober groups may provide relevant experiences. Additionally, these groups hold the alcohol addict responsible and provide a place to go in case of relapse.

Additional therapies, such as the following, may be helpful for someone with an alcohol addiction:

Drug counseling, dietary adjustments
To treat certain illnesses, a doctor may prescribe medication. For instance, if a person with an alcohol addiction self-medicates to alleviate their sadness, they may use antidepressants. Or a doctor can suggest medication to help with other feelings that are typical of healing.

Therapy may help assist someone in learning the skills necessary to handle the stress of recovery and avoid relapses. A good diet may also help reverse whatever negative effects alcohol may have had on a person's health, such as weight increase or loss.

Alcoholism treatment may entail a variety of techniques. Each individual has to enroll in a treatment program that will encourage long-term sobriety. This might include a focus on counseling for a depressed person or inpatient care for a person experiencing severe withdrawal symptoms.

What tools are available to treat alcoholism? It may be preferable to speak with a doctor for further information about alcoholism or to assist a loved one in finding choices for treatment. They might suggest nearby initiatives like 12-step groups or treatment facilities. Additionally, the following groups might be useful:

The National Council on Drug and Alcohol Dependence (NCADD)
Alcoholism Research Center at the National Institutes of Health (NIAAA)
National Institute on Drug Abuse, a Reliable Source
The Substance Abuse and Mental Health Services Administration is a reliable source.
DrugFree.org
How does alcoholism appear in the future?
The best results come from early alcoholism therapy. Long-term addictions are more difficult to overcome. Addictions that last a long time, nevertheless, may be effectively addressed.

It is possible for someone who has been abstaining from alcohol for months or years to start drinking again. Before being sober once again, they could binge drink or drink continuously for a while. Relapse, however, does not equal failure. Resuming therapy and getting back on track is crucial.

In the end, the individual with the alcohol addiction is responsible for maintaining their recovery. If the alcoholic is still drinking, it's crucial to avoid supporting damaging habits and set healthy limits. This can include stopping any financial aid or making it challenging for them to satisfy their addiction.

Try to be supportive and encouraging as a loved one of someone who is addicted to alcohol.

Chapter 4: Healing From Tobacco

Although tobacco has been around for millennia, our knowledge of the harm smoking does to the body is far more recent. For instance, smokers often pass away more than 10 years sooner than non-smokers. By deciding to stop smoking, you may improve your health.

Health professionals have associated smoking with lung cancer since at least the 1950s. More health consequences of tobacco use are being identified via research, including malignancies and chronic (long-term) disorders.

According to experts, 16 million Americans suffer from a condition brought on by smoking. Approximately 480,000 individuals every year pass away from illnesses linked to smoking. In other words, for every smoker who passes away, at least 30 more suffer from a major smoking-related ailment.

A nonprofit academic medical facility, Cleveland Clinic. Our aim is aided by the advertising on our website. We don't suggest Cleveland Clinic-exclusive goods or services. Policy

Numerous individuals think that smoking a cigar is less dangerous than smoking a cigarette. However, cigar users run into many of the same dangers as cigarette users, including cancer. Additionally, smokeless tobacco products and chewing tobacco are not any less harmful than cigarettes. There are about 30 cancer-causing compounds in smokeless tobacco.

E-cigarettes (vapes), a new method of delivering nicotine, are distinct from conventional tobacco products. In a smokeless inhaled mist, vaping offers more concentrated nicotine than cigarettes (vapor). The health hazards associated with vaping devices include cancer, chronic obstructive lung disease, and asthma.

Use of tobacco damages all of your body's organs. In addition to nicotine, smoking tobacco exposes your lungs, blood, and organs to more than 5,000 chemicals, many of which are carcinogens (chemicals that cause cancer).

Smoking-related harm may dramatically reduce your longevity. Smoking ranks first among factors that may be avoided in deaths in the US.

Smokers who are pregnant also put their unborn children in danger. Pregnancy-related side effects include:

- Ectopic pregnancy, when the embryo implants outside the uterus, is a potentially fatal disorder.
- Miscarriages.
- Stillbirths.
- Birth flaws like cleft palates.
- Low weight at birth.

Nicotine addiction may be brought on by smokeless tobacco. Chewing tobacco users run the risk of developing pancreatic, esophageal, and oral cancers. Additionally, chewing tobacco leads to tooth loss, decay, and gum disease.

E-cigarette safety and risks are yet unknown. Numerous e-cigarettes have significant nicotine content. Additionally, vaping could serve as a stepping stone for other nicotine delivery systems like cigarettes or chewing tobacco.

There are additional harmful components in the vapor of e-cigarettes. These non-nicotine vape additives may severely, perhaps fatally, harm your lungs if you breathe them in.

How are tobacco-related health issues identified?
Your particular symptoms will determine the diagnosis. For instance, a smoker who uses smokeless tobacco and gets stomach cancer after ingesting nicotine-containing juice would need different testing than a smoker.

If you smoke, your healthcare professional will inquire about your tobacco use in detail, do a physical examination on you, and sometimes prescribe tests (like an X-ray to check for organ damage or an electrocardiogram and other heart-related tests).

What additional problems might smoking exacerbate or cause?

Smoking causes a variety of additional chronic (long-term) health issues that need continuing treatment in addition to the established cancer risks. The following specific smoking-related issues need treatment:

HDL (good) cholesterol decline and blood pressure rise (increasing risks for heart attack and stroke).

erection problems.

Reduced blood flow to the heart and other bodily parts (increasing risks for coronary artery disease, peripheral artery disease, and diabetes).

Colds come on more often, particularly in kids who live with smokers.

Having a harder time getting adequate oxygen results in COPD, asthma, bronchitis, or emphysema.

How may a smoking-related illness be managed?
Most smoking-related illnesses are treatable by medical professionals. You could need

A cardiologist (heart physician) to address any heart injury.
An expert in the treatment of lung conditions like COPD
An oncology group to handle any tumors you could get.

Never starting smoking is the greatest method to prevent becoming ill from it. If you smoke, giving it up as soon as you can help you avoid or reverse health issues. If you don't smoke, you can:

- Living longer
- Lower your chance of developing cardiovascular disease.
- Lower your chance of getting some other diseases.
- Feel better and more energized.

- Feel and look better.
- Enhance your ability to taste and smell.
- Spend less.

There are several approaches to quitting smoking. Finding a smoking cessation strategy that suits your personality is essential for success. You must be intellectually and emotionally prepared. Not simply your loved ones or close acquaintances who are exposed to your secondhand smoke should be the reason you wish to stop smoking.

This advice might be helpful if you decide to stop smoking:

Get rid of any cigarettes, lighters, and other smoking-related items like ashtrays.
a smoker and a roommate? Ask them not to smoke around you or persuade them to stop smoking beside you.

Don't concentrate on the desires when they occur. Because cravings pass, concentrate on your motivation for quitting instead.

Find activities for your hands to engage in, such as doodling or toying with a pencil or straw, to keep yourself occupied. Alter all actions related to smoking as well. Instead of having a smoke, go for a stroll or read a book.

Take a big breath whenever you feel the urge to smoke. Hold it for 10 seconds, then gently let go. Repeat this numerous times until you no longer feel the want to smoke. Additionally, you might attempt meditation to lower your overall stress levels.

Avoid the people, places, and circumstances in which you identify with smoking. Spend time with non-smokers or visit locations where smoking is prohibited (like movies, museums, shops, or libraries).

Avoid replacing smoke with food or sugar-based items. These could result in weight gain. Pick healthful, low-calorie options instead. Try chewing gum, carrot or celery sticks, or hard sweets without sugar.

Limit alcohol- and caffeine-containing drinks, but be sure to stay hydrated. They may make you want to smoke.

Remind yourself that you don't smoke and that you are a nonsmoker.

Exercise is important because it helps you relax and is good for your health.

Is it too late for me to stop smoking if I've been a smoker for a while?
At any age, quitting smoking will improve your health. Smoking-related harm may be repaired over time.

Benefits accrue practically immediately after quitting:

Your blood pressure and pulse rate begin to fall after 20 minutes as the temperature of your hands and feet rises. Additionally, you stop air pollution.

Your blood will have greater quantities of oxygen and lower levels of carbon monoxide after eight hours.

Your chance of having a heart attack diminishes after 24 hours.

Your nerve endings acclimate to the lack of nicotine after 48 hours, and you start to restore your sense of taste and smell.

Your circulation becomes better after two to three months, and you can handle the additional activity.

Your general energy level rises and you cough less after one to nine months. Additionally, nasal congestion, exhaustion, and breathlessness subside.

After a year, your chance of developing heart disease is half that of a smoker.

Your risk of stroke decreases to that of non-smokers after five to fifteen years.

Your chance of dying from lung cancer decreases to virtually the same level as a lifetime nonsmoker after ten years. You also lower your chances of developing other malignancies.

Your risk of developing heart disease eventually equals that of nonsmokers after 15 years.